England Rugby

THE OFF
ENGLAND
ANNUAL 2024

Written by Calum McLaggan

Designed by Darryl Tooth

CONTENTS

2023/24 FIXTURES

MEN'S RUGBY WORLD CUP 2023

ENGLAND v ARGENTINA
Saturday 9 September at 20:00
Orange Velodrome, Marseille

ENGLAND v JAPAN
Sunday 17 September at 20:00
Allianz Riviera, Nice

ENGLAND v CHILE
Saturday 23 September at 16:45
Stade Pierre-Mauroy, Lille

ENGLAND v SAMOA
Saturday 7 October at 16:45
Stade Pierre-Mauroy, Lille

QUARTER-FINALS
Saturday 14 – Sunday 15 October

SEMI-FINALS
Friday 20 – Saturday 21 October

BRONZE FINAL & FINAL
Friday 27 – Saturday 28 October

All World Cup times are BST

MEN'S GUINNESS SIX NATIONS 2024

ITALY v ENGLAND
Saturday 3 February at 14:15
Stadio Olimpico

ENGLAND v WALES
Saturday 10 February at 16:45
Twickenham Stadium

SCOTLAND v ENGLAND
Saturday 24 February at 16:45
BT Murrayfield

ENGLAND v IRELAND
Saturday 9 March at 16:45
Twickenham Stadium

FRANCE v ENGLAND
Saturday 16 March at 20:00
Parc OL

TIKTOK WOMEN'S SIX NATIONS 2024

ITALY v ENGLAND
Sunday 24 March at 15:00

ENGLAND v WALES
Saturday 30 March at 16:45

SCOTLAND v ENGLAND
Saturday 13 April at 14:15

ENGLAND v IRELAND
Saturday 20 April at 14:15

FRANCE v ENGLAND
Saturday 27 April at 16:45
Venues still TBC

All Six Nations times (Men and Women) are GMT

WELCOME TO THE OFFICIAL ENGLAND RUGBY ANNUAL 2024

If you're a fan of England Rugby, we've got some good news: 2023/24 is going to be another bumper year with lots to look forward to!

As you read this, the men's side will have already kicked off their 2023 Rugby World Cup campaign. Can England go one better than 2019 and lift the famous Webb Ellis Cup this time? Why not! Then, three months later, the 2024 Guinness Six Nations gets underway, culminating on 16 March with a mouth-watering Saturday night showdown against France in Lyon.

The women's side, a.k.a the Red Roses, bounced back from disappointment in New Zealand with a Grand Slam in front of a record crowd at Twickenham and now have a TikTok Women's Six Nations title defence and the small matter of a home Rugby World Cup to prepare for. There are also exciting new developments in the women's game at club level, with a new-look top-flight league for the 2023/24 season.

Anyway, what better way to get yourself pumped up for a massive year of rugby than diving into our official annual, packed with fun activities, amazing facts and stats, exclusive interviews, and awesome pictures of your favourite players?

Let's do this!

MEET THE NEW BOSS

Steve Borthwick took over from Eddie Jones as England's Head Coach in December 2022, and when you look at his coaching credentials, it is easy to see why 'Borthers' - as he's also known - was chosen for the top job.

At club level, he coached Saracens and Leicester Tigers, where he won the 2021/22 Premiership title and oversaw the club's best winning run for 25 years. At international level, he worked with Japan, the British & Irish Lions and England, where he was Forwards Coach between 2015 and 2020.

A new Head Coach with a clear vision and a dynamic young team at his fingertips: exciting times ahead, England fans!

BORTHWICK 'THE PLAYER'

You know Steve Borthwick, the head coach. But what about Steve Borthwick, the player? Here are some facts you might not know about the former England skipper.

- *He started playing rugby at Preston Grasshoppers.*
- *He played in the second row.*
- *Before becoming a full international, he represented England Schools, Colts and Saxons.*
- *He made his Test debut against France at Twickenham in 2001.*
- *He went on to play 57 Tests for England, finishing in 2010.*
- *He captained England 21 times.*
- *He played at Bath for ten years and at Saracens for six, where he won the Premiership in 2011.*
- *He made 265 Premiership appearances - a record at the time.*

"I want to build a winning team which inspires young people to fall in love with Rugby Union the way I did. I want the whole country to be proud of us and to enjoy watching us play."

2023 GUINNESS SIX NATIONS CHAMPIONSHIP

Ireland went into the 2023 Guinness Six Nations ranked as No. 1 in the world, and boy did they back it up, winning all five matches and storming their way to a Grand Slam in Dublin. Congratulations to the men in green.

How about England? Well, while two wins from five doesn't sound great, it's worth remembering that Steve Borthwick only came into the role six weeks before the start of the tournament, and - just like starting a new school or joining a new rugby club - it takes time to adapt.

There were plenty of positives to take from the tournament, though, as well as some stand-out performances from England's up-and-coming stars. One thing's for sure: the 2023 Six Nations was an invaluable learning experience ahead of the Rugby World Cup in France.

England kicked off their Six Nations campaign with a six-point thriller against Scotland, but despite a massive effort from the boys, the Calcutta Cup will be staying in Edinburgh for another year.

Max Malins bagged a well-taken brace in the first half, but the match will be remembered for a moment of brilliance from Duhan van der Merwe, who slalomed his way over from 60 metres out to score a try that was later voted the Guinness Six Nations Try of the Championship. Ellis Genge crashed over to put England in front shortly after the restart, but further scores from Ben White, and a second from van der Merwe, put Scotland on the path to victory.

The result might not have gone our way, but it was great to see Dan Cole pull on an England jersey for the first time since 2019... and who could forget the sight of the Leicester Tigers prop coming off the bench in the 60th minute, going straight into a scrum, and winning a penalty? Now that's what you call instant impact!

ENGLAND	**23**
SCOTLAND	**29**

Twickenham Stadium, 4 February

ENGLAND 31
ITALY 14

Twickenham Stadium, 12 February

What's the best way to get over a disappointing defeat? Work hard in training and bounce back with a win: and that's just what England did eight days later at Twickenham, scoring five tries in a bonus-point victory against an ever-improving Italy side.

England's power play up front was irresistible, with close-range scores from Jack Willis, Jamie George and a first test try for Ollie Chessum, as Steve Borthwick's side took a 19-point lead into the break. Despite conceding a penalty try early in the second half, Italy rallied with scores from Marco Riccioni and Alessandro Fusco. But there was no way England were going to let this one slip.

The decisive moment came in the 71st minute, when scrum-half Alex Mitchell, having come on for his England debut, snuck round the blindside from ten metres out and fed Henry Arundell, who sealed the win with a slick finish in the corner – much to the delight of a packed-out Twickenham.

Italian job: done ✓ Next assignment: Wales in Cardiff.

WALES 10
ENGLAND 20

Principality Stadium, 25 February

No matter what the result is, Wales vs England is always an occasion to remember. The 2023 Six Nations meeting between the two sides would prove no different, with Steve Borthwick's boys banking England's first win in Cardiff in six years.

England started brightly and raced into an eight-point lead inside 20 minutes with a long-range penalty from Owen Farrell, followed by an acrobatic touchline finish from Anthony Watson.

Trailing 3-8 at the start of the second half, this time it was Wales' turn to make a quick start from kick-off, and when livewire wing Louis Rees-Zammit intercepted a loose pass, sprinted under the posts, and Halfpenny converted, the men in red soon found themselves two points up.

Roared on by noisy travelling support, England trucked the ball upfield after the restart and pummelled the Wales defence with carry after powerful carry, before Kyle Sinckler eventually barged his way over the line to restore England's lead. Heading into the closing stages, England went on the hunt for a match-winning try and found it when Alex Mitchell recycled the ball quickly from a ruck, and Ollie Lawrence darted over from close range to seal the victory.

There's no such thing as an easy test match in Cardiff, and captain Owen Farrell was relieved to get the win: *"We came here to do a job, and we've done it. We stuck in there, fought until the end, and I think we took control of that last 20 minutes."*

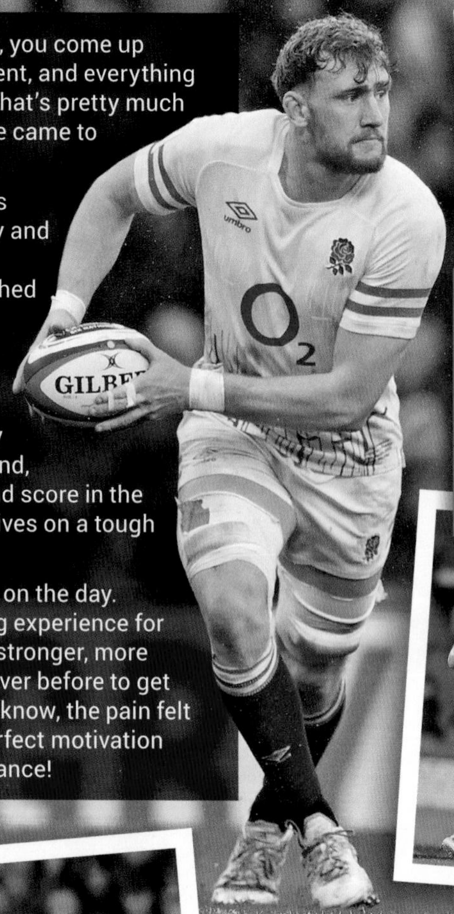

Every now and then in rugby, you come up against a formidable opponent, and everything clicks for them on the day. That's pretty much what happened when France came to Twickenham in Round Four.

As the scoreline suggests, the visitors were by far the better team on the day and took just two minutes to get on the scoreboard when Tomas Ramos finished off a blistering counter-attack in the corner. Ramos was one of three French players to score a double on the day, alongside Thibaud Flament (formerly of Loughborough University 4ths!) and Damian Penaud. For England, Freddie Steward's well-taken carry and score in the 48th minute was one of the few positives on a tough afternoon at Twickenham.

France were at their scintillating best on the day. While this was a bitterly disappointing experience for England, matches like this make you stronger, more resilient, and more determined than ever before to get back to winning ways. And you never know, the pain felt from a result like this could be the perfect motivation heading into a Rugby World Cup in France!

ENGLAND 10
FRANCE 53

Twickenham Stadium, 11 March

IRELAND 29
ENGLAND 16

Aviva Stadium, 18 March

England's final assignment saw them travel to the Aviva Stadium in Dublin, with Ireland on the brink of clinching a home Grand Slam. The build-up for both sides heading into this one couldn't have been more different. While England had suffered a record home defeat against France just seven days before, Andy Farrell's side went into their Grand Slam decider having won 21 of their previous 23 tests. No prizes for guessing who the pre-match favourites were!

A foregone conclusion, then? No chance!

England started brightly, hitting the breakdown at speed, piling on the pressure up front, and even taking a six-point lead through two coolly-taken Owen Farrell penalties. Ireland responded with three points from Jonny Sexton - a strike that saw him become the all-time leading points scorer in the Six Nations - and a Dan Sheehan try. Then, with the clock ticking down to half time, Freddie Steward clattered into Hugo Keenan, a red card was brandished, and England would have to face Ireland with 14 men for the second year in a row.

Despite the numerical disadvantage, Steve Borthwick's boys showed plenty of spirit in the second half and can be proud that they were just one point down with 19 minutes to go. In the end, though, the pressure became too much, and the hosts pulled away with three tries in the closing stages, while Jamie George grabbed a late consolation score for England.

Defeat in Dublin, but massive credit to the boys who pushed the No. 1 ranked side in the world all the way under challenging circumstances. Congratulations to Ireland: Grand Slam winners in Dublin for the first time in their history.

Must have been some party afterwards!

ELLIS GENGE

A powerful and dynamic prop, the 'Baby Rhino' has been one of the stand-out performers for club and country over the last couple of years. A natural-born leader, Ellis was named England captain for the first time during the 2023 Guinness Six Nations, wearing the skipper's armband against France at Twickenham.

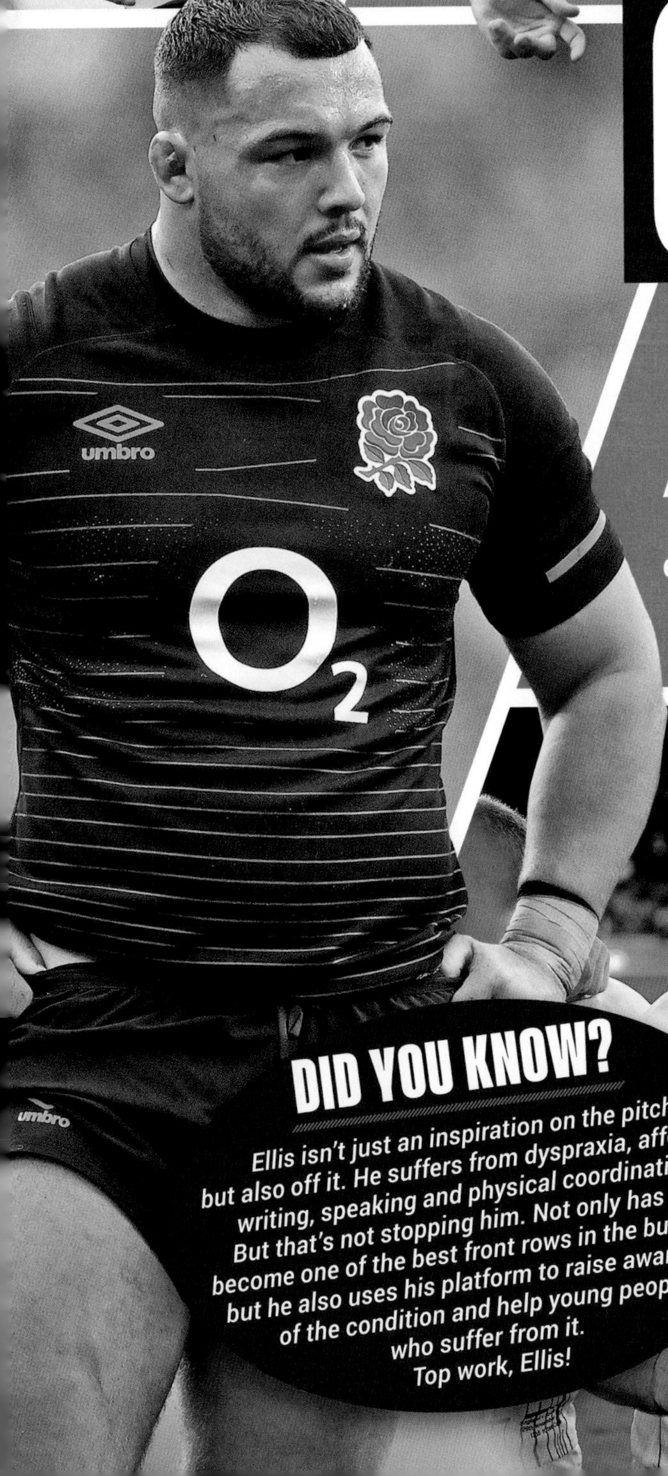

DID YOU KNOW?

Ellis isn't just an inspiration on the pitch but also off it. He suffers from dyspraxia, affecting writing, speaking and physical coordination. But that's not stopping him. Not only has Ellis become one of the best front rows in the business, but he also uses his platform to raise awareness of the condition and help young people who suffer from it. Top work, Ellis!

ENGLAND'S SET PIECE POWER

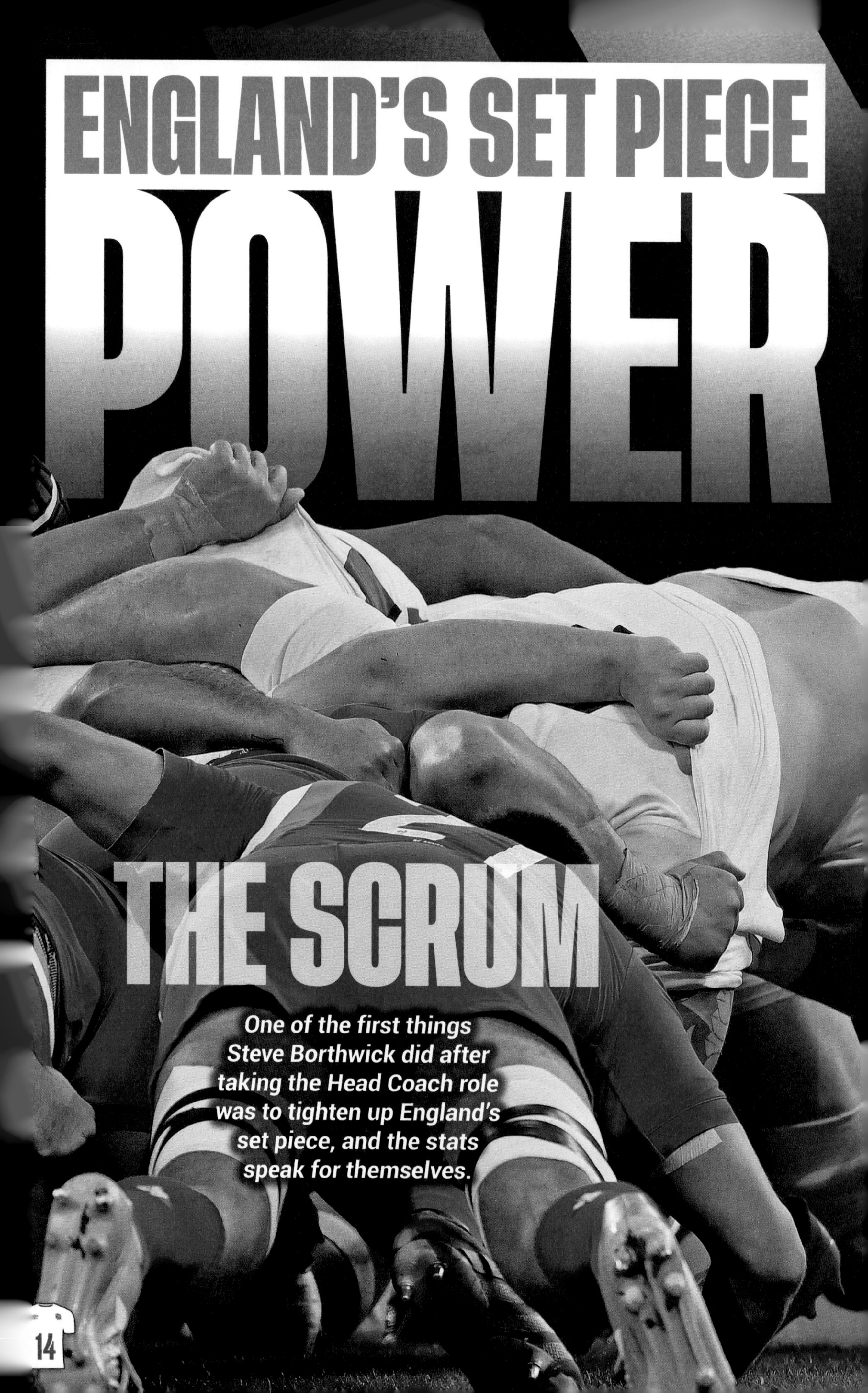

THE SCRUM

One of the first things Steve Borthwick did after taking the Head Coach role was to tighten up England's set piece, and the stats speak for themselves.

THE LINEOUT

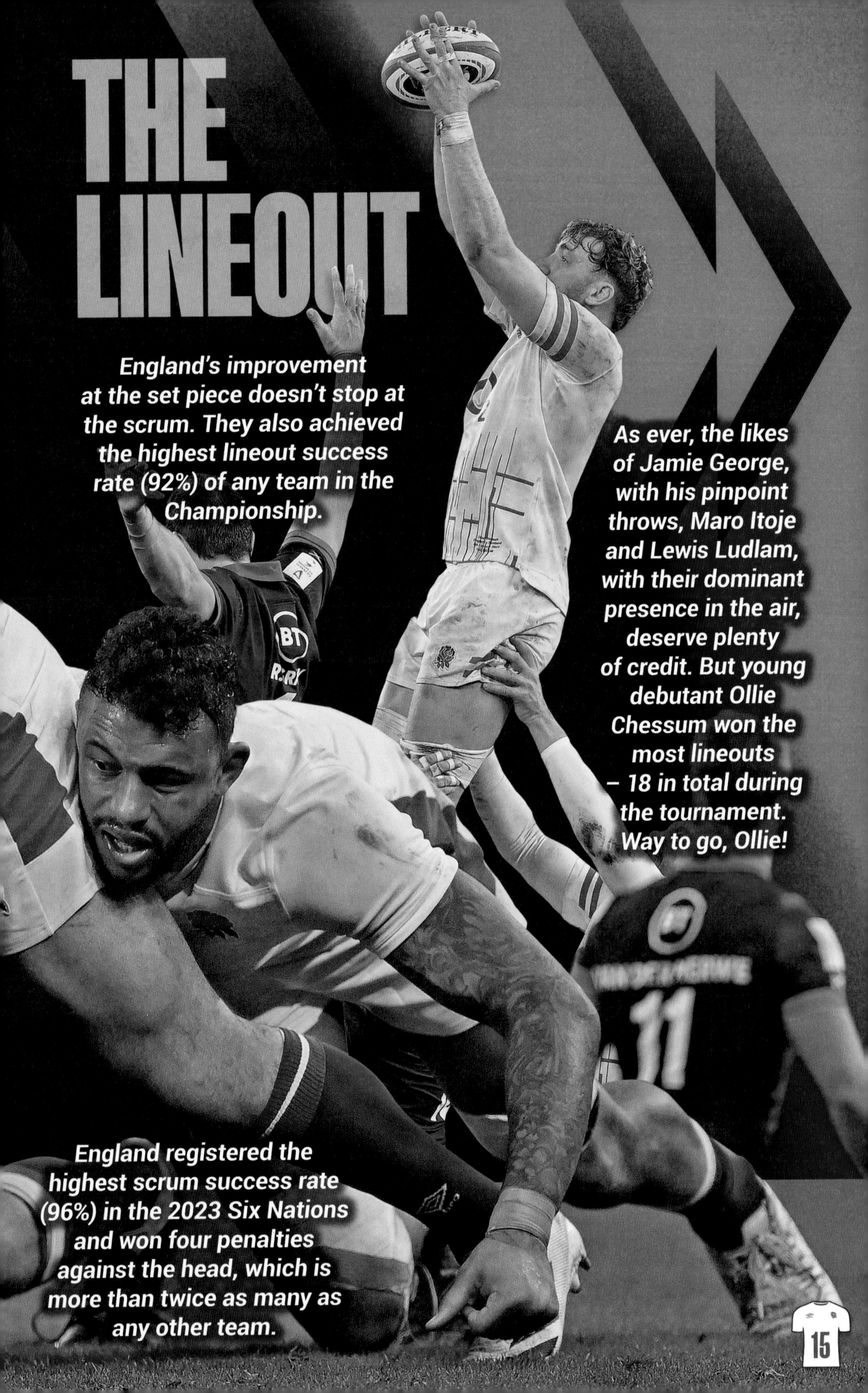

England's improvement at the set piece doesn't stop at the scrum. They also achieved the highest lineout success rate (92%) of any team in the Championship.

As ever, the likes of Jamie George, with his pinpoint throws, Maro Itoje and Lewis Ludlam, with their dominant presence in the air, deserve plenty of credit. But young debutant Ollie Chessum won the most lineouts – 18 in total during the tournament. Way to go, Ollie!

England registered the highest scrum success rate (96%) in the 2023 Six Nations and won four penalties against the head, which is more than twice as many as any other team.

OLLIE LAWRENCE

The explosive centre has enjoyed a new lease of life since joining Bath and even scooped the 2022/23 Gallagher Premiership Player of the Season Award. 23-year-old Ollie is an admirer of Manu Tuilagi, and it's easy to see similarities in their playing styles. If recent form is anything to go by, you'll be seeing plenty more of Ollie with a Red Rose on his chest over the coming years.

DID YOU KNOW?

Ollie played for the Academies at Aston Villa and Birmingham City as a youngster before switching sports. It's safe to say that football's loss is rugby's gain!

JACK VAN POORTVLIET

Talk about 'making an entrance'... The Leicester Tigers scrum half burst onto the international scene on the 2022 tour to Australia, scoring a try just minutes after coming on for his debut against the Wallabies. Renowned for his lightning-quick passing ability and pinpoint kicking, Jack has also been praised for his leadership qualities around the breakdown: not bad for a youngster of 22.

DID YOU KNOW?

Jack grew up on a family farm in Norfolk where he spent hours copying his hero, Jonny Wilkinson, by taking penalties using a set of old rugby posts rescued from his local club, North Walsham RFC.

THE AMAZING RUGBY WORDSEARCH

Put your detective skills to the test with our Rugby Wordsearch. Can you find all 20 rugby terms in the grid below? Words can go horizontally, vertically or diagonally in all eight directions. Good luck!

Z	G	E	G	Z	S	R	A	X	K	V	L	E	L	L	I	S	G	E	N	G	E	T	F	L	M	M	O	K
M	V	Y	K	R	K	P	T	N	W	I	D	P	T	K	F	K	Y	Z	J	C	W	V	Z	T	X	Q	R	G
S	T	I	E	Q	Q	R	W	T	R	I	M	O	U	V	D	A	Q	T	N	C	X	C	R	C	K	S	J	A
O	F	E	G	Z	N	W	W	M	Q	U	M	J	R	F	D	D	Y	E	I	K	S	U	F	J	E	L	D	W
Z	B	G	J	O	R	T	Q	C	W	Z	B	N	N	U	H	C	T	Q	N	R	Z	A	Z	C	P	R	G	S
Q	Z	H	O	F	B	I	O	Q	S	M	A	W	O	U	W	I	R	L	C	N	V	A	R	H	A	F	S	I
Y	E	N	H	W	A	A	U	L	A	M	A	M	V	M	C	S	I	I	S	I	L	Z	J	W	M	L	M	B
Z	X	X	N	K	T	Z	P	G	S	S	F	U	E	I	B	R	D	P	E	V	D	C	E	I	J	I	O	X
Z	Z	X	M	E	I	U	Z	E	C	L	B	W	R	P	P	D	U	M	C	V	K	T	S	P	W	U	H	I
O	V	M	I	D	J	F	N	L	F	L	I	T	L	Z	F	X	I	H	T	T	S	B	Z	Z	V	D	U	Q
E	L	A	T	K	H	I	R	W	T	K	Z	S	A	C	L	T	H	A	I	E	D	H	V	N	W	V	N	W
A	H	F	C	S	L	A	H	X	M	Z	V	A	U	R	L	R	H	B	I	V	M	W	U	O	B	L	T	B
L	Q	Y	H	J	K	D	S	N	V	S	O	I	U	L	O	R	G	D	F	Q	S	M	Q	X	L	Z	H	W
D	J	L	E	A	R	I	C	J	N	V	U	P	U	N	D	Z	D	O	W	E	N	F	A	R	R	E	L	L
C	Q	T	L	L	Q	A	W	A	X	Y	V	F	E	U	V	E	S	C	H	A	M	P	I	O	N	S	Z	Z
R	Z	T	L	T	D	E	R	S	V	G	P	O	K	H	R	Z	W	O	R	L	D	R	E	C	O	R	D	E
O	J	B	Q	W	I	V	B	P	P	C	K	F	L	F	E	T	F	D	T	P	E	U	E	Z	W	H	E	E
F	J	M	S	A	D	I	A	K	A	B	E	Y	A	U	U	Q	E	Q	T	J	I	F	H	R	J	K	T	B
T	L	Q	W	J	Y	H	L	S	R	R	L	B	H	B	F	W	F	I	O	J	K	C	J	O	Q	P	B	V
S	E	H	F	M	V	V	D	Z	B	R	Z	Y	E	E	D	I	E	J	E	C	G	A	X	L	I	Y	D	I
J	S	Q	B	U	I	B	F	N	Q	V	P	D	P	E	N	A	L	T	Y	P	B	V	B	O	T	C	S	S
Q	K	I	C	K	O	F	F	G	D	C	W	V	F	W	J	O	J	P	D	O	Y	J	P	L	S	X	W	B
R	R	B	Y	J	I	W	G	R	A	N	D	S	L	A	M	U	K	M	M	D	F	D	G	G	Q	D	T	G
S	Z	J	B	P	N	H	A	S	T	E	V	E	B	O	R	T	H	W	I	C	K	F	L	P	F	B	I	G
C	A	P	T	A	I	N	N	K	D	R	E	D	R	O	S	E	S	L	V	M	Y	C	J	Y	Q	L	H	V
J	D	X	C	X	V	Z	B	A	L	L	B	H	R	O	K	V	H	F	M	G	B	Q	U	G	M	T	L	O
W	H	T	M	M	G	D	U	E	Y	H	S	F	G	I	I	K	L	I	I	S	O	L	R	C	I	D	H	E

Steve Borthwick	Captain	Debut	Zoe Aldcroft
Linesman	Ellis Genge	John Mitchell	Mo Hunt
Kick Off	Freddie Steward	Grand Slam	Red Roses
Full Time	Turnover	World Record	Ball
Owen Farrell	Penalty	Sadia Kabeya	Champions

WHO AM I?

Think you know England's stars? Let's put your knowledge to the test. See if you can identify this England regular from the clues below...

FACT 1
I made my England debut against the USA in 2021

FACT 2
I'm 6ft 5, but play in the backs

FACT 3
I can be called upon to kick long-range penalties

FACT 4
I studied Economics at Loughborough University

FACT 5
I play for Leicester Tigers

FACT 6
If you go to a rugby match, you might see my surname on the back of some people's jackets

ANSWER:

STILL NOT SURE? CHECK OUT THE ANSWER ON PAGE 60

WOMEN'S RUGBY

RED HOT ROSES

England went into Rugby World Cup 2022 (postponed from 2021 due to Covid) as the pre-tournament favourites, having just smashed through an astonishing 25-match record winning streak. Add to that the amazing array of talent at England's disposal, including reigning World Rugby Player of the Year, Zoe Aldcroft, and it's easy to see why the Red Roses were the team to avoid in New Zealand.

POOL STAGES

The Red Roses stormed their way through the pool stages with three wins from three, kicking their campaign off with a 14-try win against Fiji before passing a tough test against France in their second game. England's pack were super powerful against South Africa, with 12 of their 13 tries coming through the forwards and the likes of Sadia Kabeya and Hannah Botterman catching the eye with stand-out performances.

FIJI 19-84 ENGLAND

FRANCE 7-13 ENGLAND

ENGLAND 75-0 SOUTH AFRICA

WORLD CUP REVIEW

KNOCK-OUT STAGES

ENGLAND 41-5 AUSTRALIA

First up: Australia. Given the torrential rain at the Waitakere Stadium that day, this was always going to be tough. With players from both sides skidding across the grass, England kept it tight and scored seven tries, including a hat-trick from the irrepressible Marlie Packer, as the Red Roses powered past the Wallaroos and into the last four.

CANADA 19-26 ENGLAND

England's semi-final clash against Canada turned out to be a real nailbiter. Marlie Packer and Abby Dow gave England an early lead, but Canada hit back before half time to cut the gap to three points. Then, six minutes after the restart, the Red Roses scored one of the finest tries you'll ever see on a rugby pitch, as Claudia MacDonald broke from inside the dead ball area and sped upfield before releasing Abby Dow, who hit the afterburners with an astonishing turn of pace, glided past two tacklers, and over in the corner. No wonder they call her 'Abby Wow'!

THE FINAL

NEW ZEALAND 34-31 ENGLAND

And so it came to the final, against the hosts, New Zealand. A record 42,579-strong crowd packed out Eden Park, while - back home - 1.8 million of you set your alarms early to cheer on the Red Roses on ITV. An end-to-end first half saw England take a 26-19 lead, but the task got even more challenging when Lydia Thompson was shown a red card for a high tackle in the 18th minute.

The Black Ferns sprung into life in the second half, unleashing their back line and eventually edging into the lead for the first time in the 72nd minute through Ayesha Leti-I'iga. Then with the clock in the red and England camped in their opponents' 22, the Black Ferns intercepted a 5-metre lineout throw, and England's last chance of glory was gone. Heartbreak for the Red Roses, who gave it everything from start to finish, but one thing's for sure: we couldn't be prouder of them.

Congratulations to New Zealand for putting on a brilliant tournament and becoming the first-ever host nation to win the Women's Rugby World Cup.

SIMON MIDDLETON'S

AMAZING RECORD WITH THE RED ROSES

Few coaches in world rugby have ever enjoyed the level of success that Simon Middleton had with the Red Roses. Here's a look back at some of the incredible numbers from his reign as England's head coach.

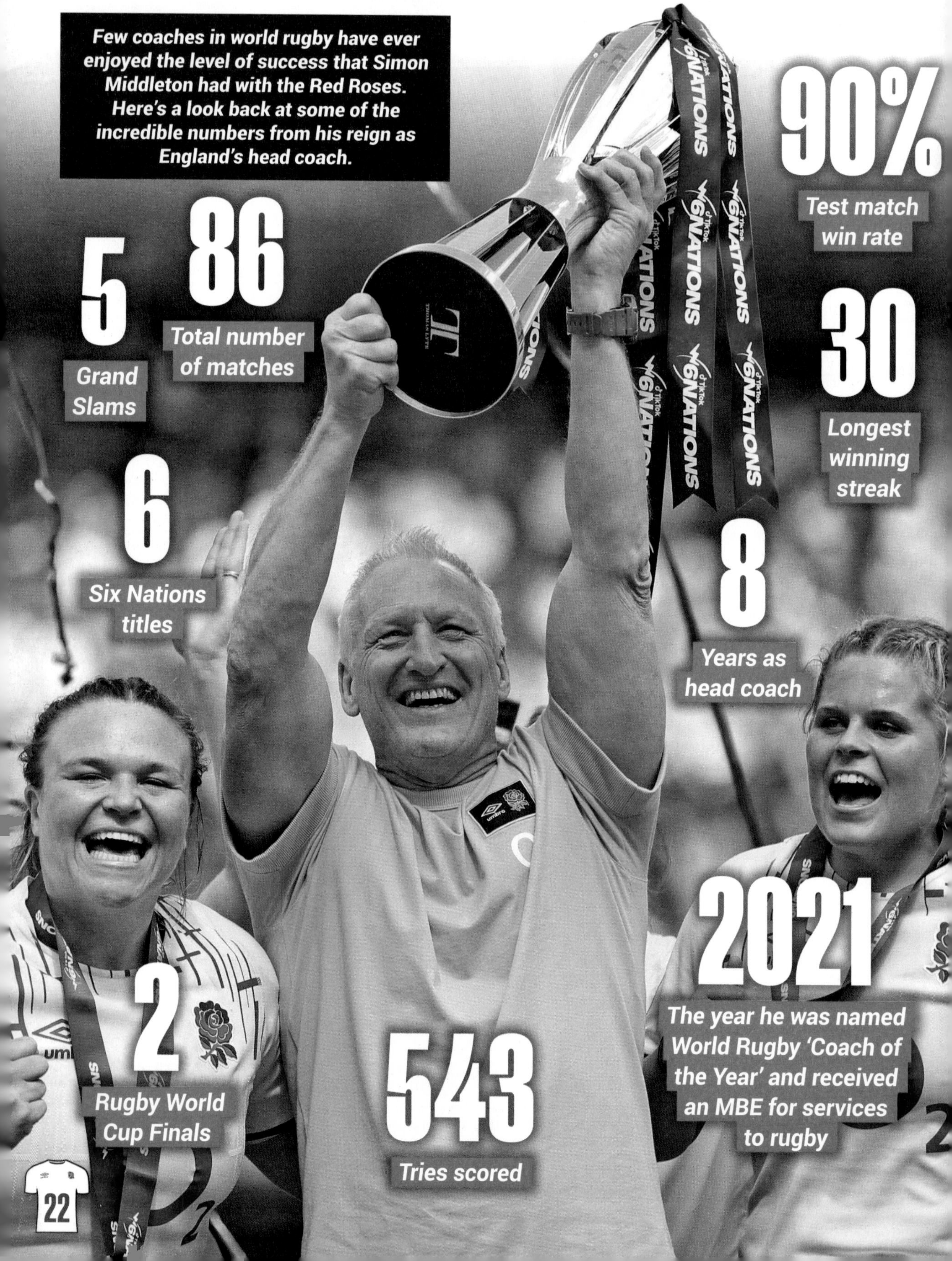

5
Grand Slams

86
Total number of matches

90%
Test match win rate

30
Longest winning streak

6
Six Nations titles

8
Years as head coach

2
Rugby World Cup Finals

543
Tries scored

2021
The year he was named World Rugby 'Coach of the Year' and received an MBE for services to rugby

MEET THE NEW BOSS

JOHN MITCHELL

Here are five things you need to know about incoming head coach John Mitchell, who will take charge of the Red Roses after the Men's Rugby World Cup in 2023.

- *59-year-old John is from Hawera in New Zealand.*
- *He will join the Red Roses from the Japan Men's team, where he is the defence coach.*
- *He has also coached in New Zealand, Australia, South Africa, USA... and England.*
- *He was head coach of the All Blacks when England won the Rugby World Cup in 2003.*
- *He worked with the England Men's team as forwards coach between 1997-2000 and defence coach between 2018-2021.*

2023 TIKTOK WOMEN'S SIX NATIONS

England went into the 2023 TikTok Women's Six Nations looking to secure an impressive fifth straight title and give head coach Simon Middleton the perfect send-off after eight years at the helm.

England's Six Nations rivals have all made significant progress on and off the field in recent years, with Scotland, Wales and Ireland boasting several star players at top clubs in the Women's Premiership Rugby, and Italy going from strength to strength.

As for France? Well, the Red Roses won the 2022 Grand Slam with a 12-24 victory against Les Bleus in Bayonne and, once again, the tournament schedule would see the two heavyweights go head-to-head on the last day of the championship. But this time, the much-anticipated showdown would take place at none other than Twickenham Stadium.

As send-offs go, this was one to remember for captain Sarah Hunter in her home town of Newcastle. After an astonishing career spanning 141 caps, nine Grand Slams and a World Cup, England's all-time record cap-holder led her country out one last time for the Red Roses' opener. As you can imagine, there were some emotional scenes for such a special occasion.

Wearing names on the back of their shirts for the first time, the Red Roses were at their dazzling best, running in 10 tries, with Claudia MacDonald and Amy Cokayne bagging two tries each and Player of the Match, Marlie Packer, clinching a hat-trick.

ENGLAND 58
SCOTLAND 7

Kingston Park, 25 March 2023

ENGLAND 68
ITALY 5

Franklin's Gardens, 2 April 2023

Nearly 13,000 fans packed into Franklin's Gardens for England's next match against Italy. After the two sides traded early tries, it was largely one-way traffic toward the Italian line, as the Red Roses backed up their performance against Scotland with an equally impressive display in Round Two.

England's back line were in devastating form all afternoon, with Jessica Breach adding two more to seal her hat-trick, MacDonald making it back-to-back doubles and speedster Abby Dow running in four tries. The Red Roses ran Italy ragged, scoring 12 tries in total and carrying over 1,000 metres in 80 minutes. Now that's a good day's work!

WALES 3
ENGLAND 59

Cardiff Arms Park, 15 April 2023

With two home victories in the bag, it was time to take that winning run on the road. Wales came into this fixture in fine form, having secured back-to-back wins in their opening two matches, and had a chance to seal a Triple Crown in front of a sold-out crowd in Cardiff. The hosts more than held their own for the first half hour, taking the lead early on through a Keira Bevan penalty and keeping England away from the tryline until the 27th minute, when Lucy Packer darted over. But with the clock ticking down to half time, Dow produced a moment of magic, weaving her way past six defenders to score the try of the tournament. England didn't take their foot off the gas after the restart, either, and ran in nine unanswered tries in total to keep their hopes of a Grand Slam firmly on track.

England came out firing in Cork, taking just two minutes to get on the scoresheet via Sarah Beckett, and bringing up the bonus point inside 26 minutes through Marlie Packer. Trailing 0-27 at the break, Ireland rallied well and managed to keep England from scoring again until the 71st minute when Amber Reed dotted down her first try of the tournament, and Alex Matthews followed that up with two scores in quick succession.

Despite the emphatic scoreline, this was, in truth, a scrappy encounter, with both sides far from their best. Among the positives for England was the return of Natasha 'Mo' Hunt, who, having missed out on Rugby World Cup 2022 selection, made her long-awaited return from injury: *"It feels bittersweet,"* said Mo after the game, *"because we're very frustrated with how we went about it, but I am so proud to be back with the girls. It's such an honour to play for your country and get another shot to pull the jersey on."*

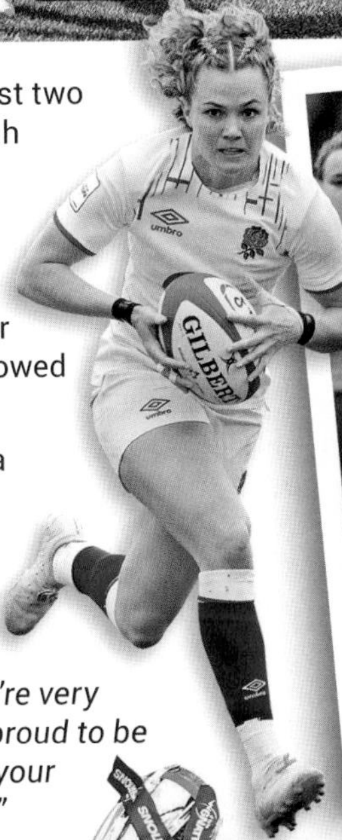

IRELAND 0
ENGLAND 48

Musgrave Park, 22 April 2023

ENGLAND 38
FRANCE 33

Twickenham Stadium, 29 April 2023

Cue the 2023 Grand Slam decider and a historic day for women's rugby at Twickenham.

England were dominant throughout the first half, racking up five tries before the break through Abby Dow, Marlie Packer, Alex Matthews, Zoe Aldcroft and a penalty try, with the visitors even going down to 13 players at one point after picking up two yellow cards.

To France's credit, they never gave up and hammered away at England after the restart, cutting the deficit with two well-taken tries. Lark Davies stemmed the fightback with a powerful score from close-range, before France hit back with another try. Then, in the 71st minute came the announcement that everyone had been waiting for: *"Today's official attendance is 58,498,"* boomed the stadium loudspeaker, *"A new world record for a women's rugby match!"* It was a special moment, celebrated in the stands like a match-winning try.

France finished with a flurry and ran in two last-gasp tries. But, while the final score was a little too close for comfort, it was another professional job from the Red Roses, who gave departing head coach Simon Middleton the perfect leaving gift: a Grand Slam at Twickenham.

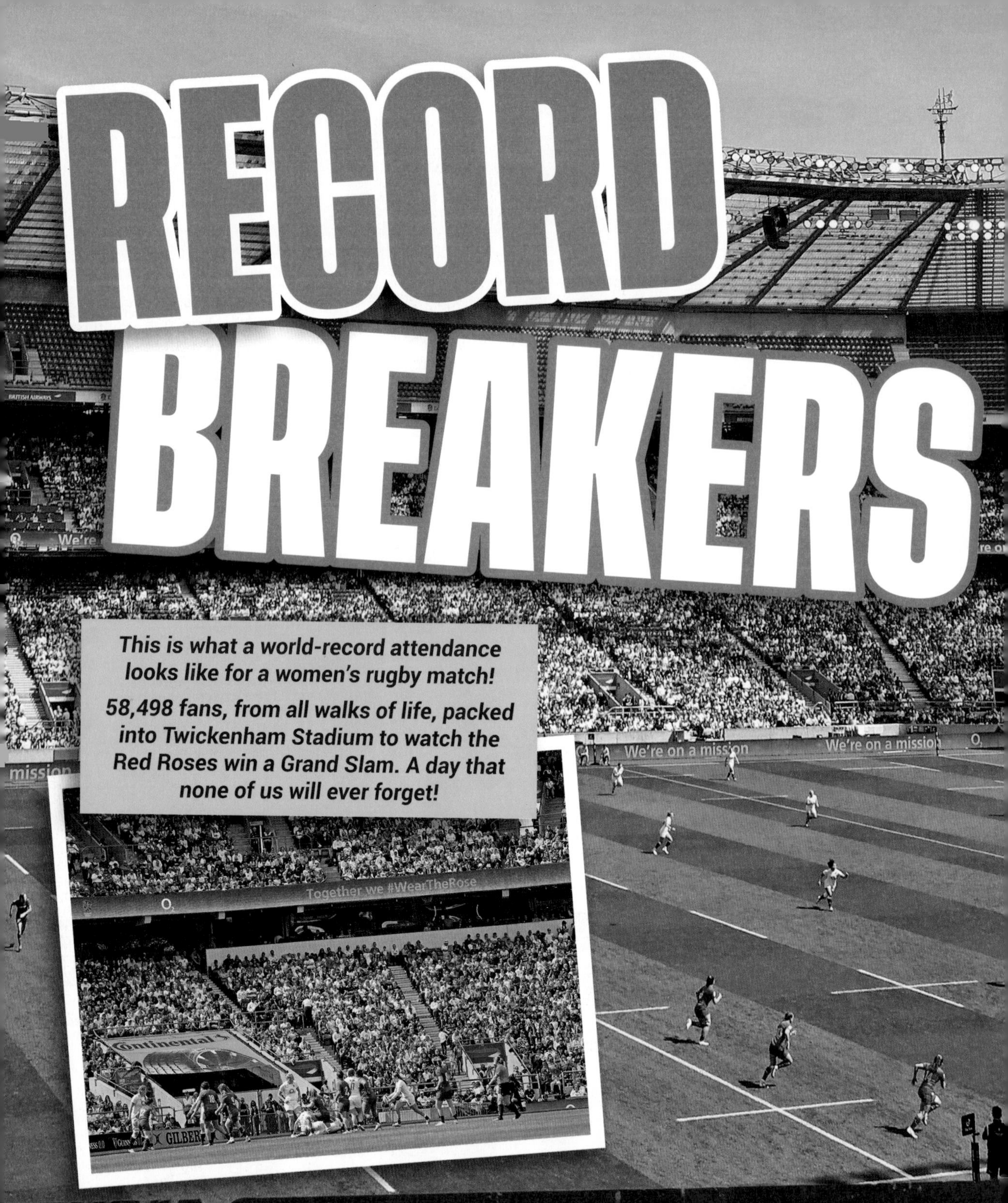

RECORD BREAKERS

This is what a world-record attendance looks like for a women's rugby match!

58,498 fans, from all walks of life, packed into Twickenham Stadium to watch the Red Roses win a Grand Slam. A day that none of us will ever forget!

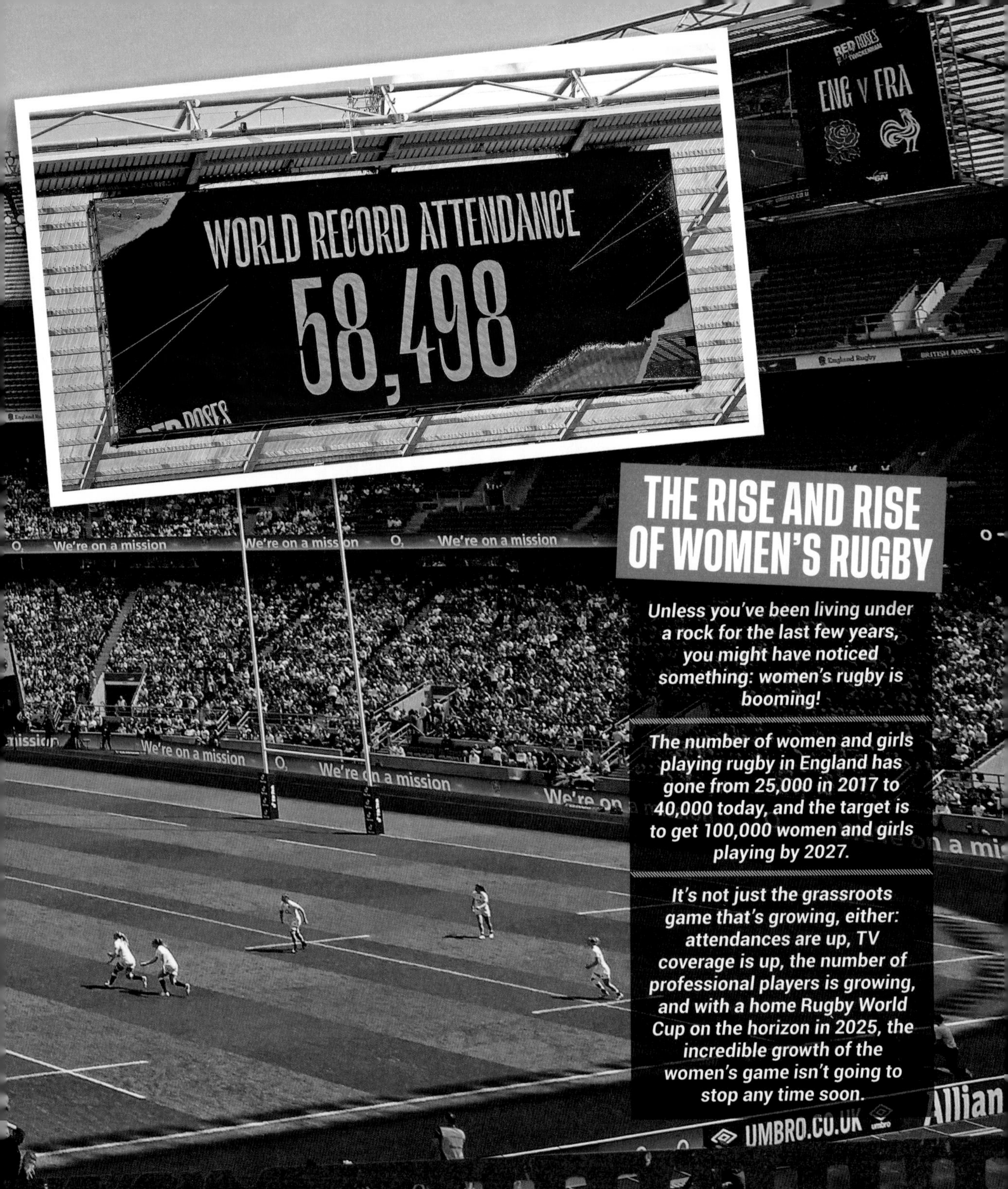

THE RISE AND RISE OF WOMEN'S RUGBY

Unless you've been living under a rock for the last few years, you might have noticed something: women's rugby is booming!

The number of women and girls playing rugby in England has gone from 25,000 in 2017 to 40,000 today, and the target is to get 100,000 women and girls playing by 2027.

It's not just the grassroots game that's growing, either: attendances are up, TV coverage is up, the number of professional players is growing, and with a home Rugby World Cup on the horizon in 2025, the incredible growth of the women's game isn't going to stop any time soon.

TATYANA HEARD

The Gloucester-Hartpury centre was a key part of the Red Roses' 2023 Grand Slam win, scoring in four of England's five tests. Tatyana also posted some impressive stats, racking up 297 metres, 29 tackles and 31 carries during the campaign.

DID YOU KNOW?

Tatyana was born in Pisa, Italy, before moving to Maryland, USA, and then Kirkbymoorside in North Yorkshire, where she grew up. Talk about well-travelled!

HOLLY AITCHISON

Whether she's pulling the strings at fly half, or dancing through defenders in midfield, there are few back line players more versatile or lethal than Holly Aitchison. The former Saracen switched to number 10 early on in the 2022/23 season after an unfortunate injury to teammate Zoe Harrison and more than stepped up to the task, starting every Six Nations match at fly half en route to the Grand Slam.

DID YOU KNOW?

Holly played for England Sevens before making the switch to 15s. In fact, she was so impressive on the World Rugby Sevens circuit that she was even selected to represent Great Britain at the 2020 Olympics in Tokyo!

SPOTLIGHT ON: SADIA KABEYA

22-year-old Loughborough Lightning flanker, Sadia Kabeya, has enjoyed a meteoric rise through the ranks.

From discovering rugby at secondary school to winning a 2023 Grand Slam with the Red Roses and everything in between, Sadia spoke to Alfie Martin about her rugby journey.

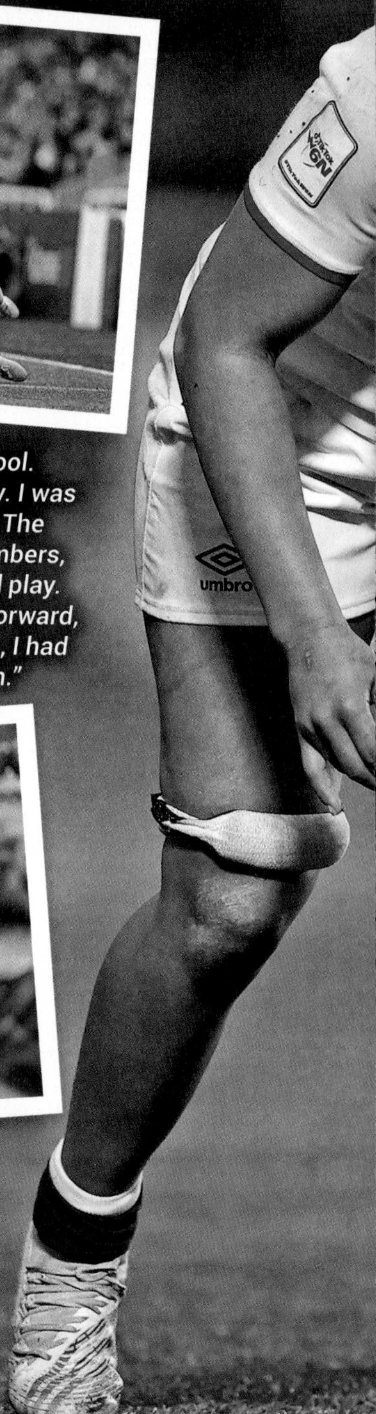

DISCOVERING RUGBY

"I first started playing rugby in secondary school. I was in year eight, and I'd always been very sporty. I was in a science lesson and got pulled out of class. The teacher said that the rugby team were low on numbers, that they had some spare kit and asked if I would play. I didn't know the rules; they just said I had to run forward, pass backwards, and that was it. After saying yes, I had to look for some boots in the lost property bin."

NEW BALLS PLEASE

"I was quite an aggressive child when it came to sport. I remember trying to play tennis and it was a no-go because I would just whack the ball out of the court every single time. They evidently thought rugby would be good for me."

LOVE AT FIRST SIGHT

"I had such a great time, and it was great to play a sport with my friends that I hadn't played before. When the game finished, everyone was saying 'wow, Sadia, you were really good!', and in my head I was just thinking that I'd done what they told me to do. I fell in love with rugby straight away."

COACH CLEALL

"Bryony Cleall joined our school two years later, and I'd been playing at school casually for a couple of years. She was in the England setup at the time and she encouraged me to take up rugby outside school and pursue it seriously. Before, it was just a pastime and an excuse to get out of lessons, but Bry showed me that it could be a career path."

JOINING RICHMOND RUGBY

"I remember being extremely nervous, and I'd shy away from doing any carrying. Any time I could get on the inside and get away with not being the ball carrier, I would. Tackling has always been my thing, and in that game, I realised that if I got low enough, I could get them down. That's really where my love for the game came from, and the realisation of what my strengths were."

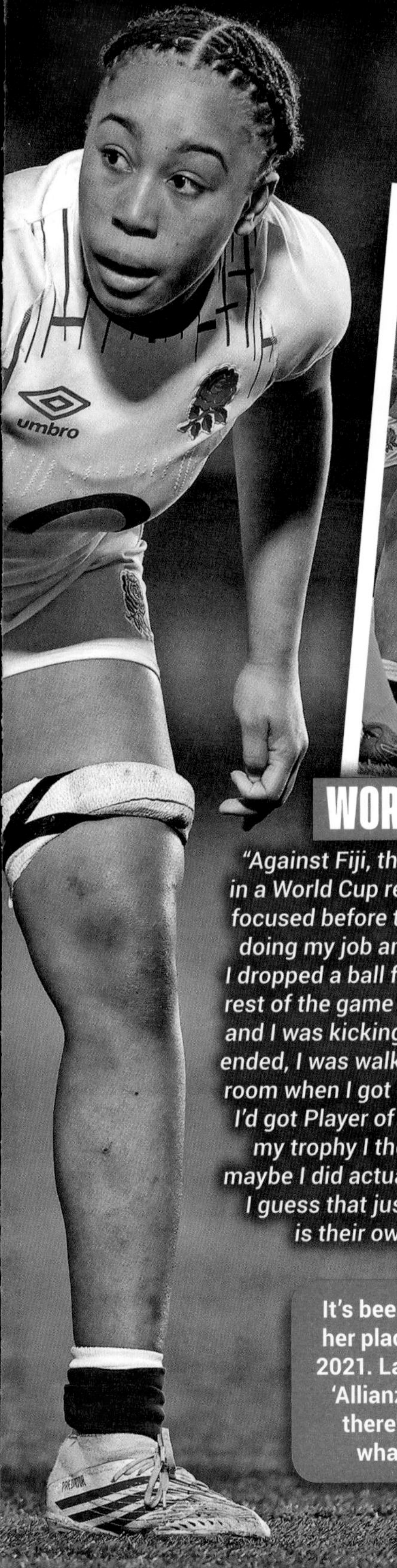

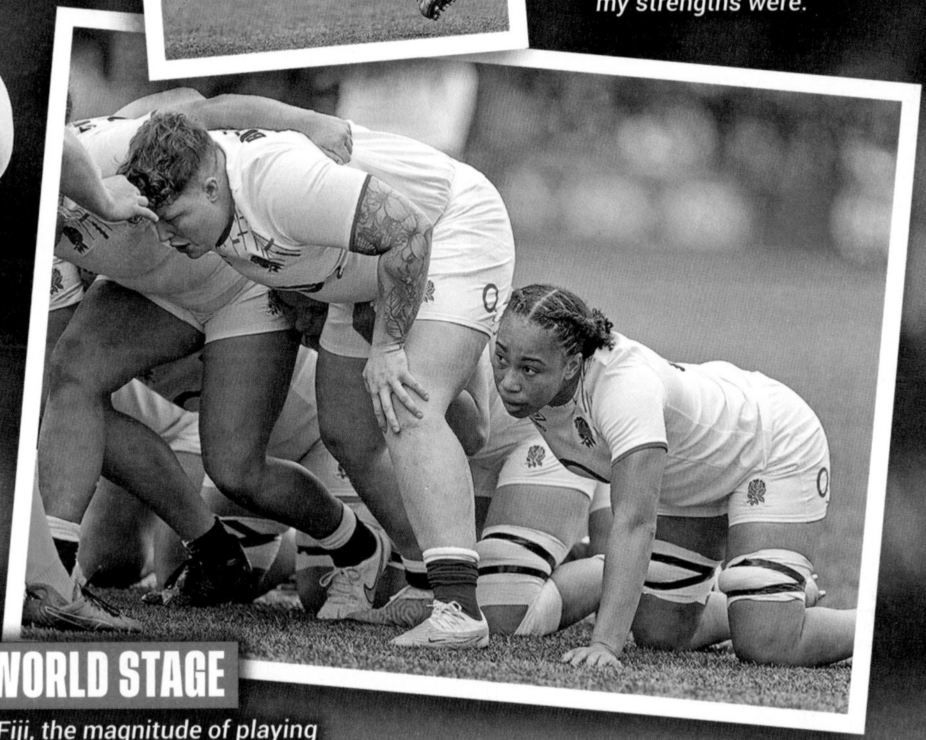

WORLD STAGE

"Against Fiji, the magnitude of playing in a World Cup really hit me. I was hyper-focused before the game thinking about doing my job and having a good game. I dropped a ball from a kick-off, so for the rest of the game that's all I could think of, and I was kicking myself. When the game ended, I was walking back to the changing room when I got pulled back and was told I'd got Player of the Match. Going to get my trophy I thought to myself 'Okay, maybe I did actually have a decent game'. I guess that just shows that everyone is their own harshest critic."

ENGLAND CALL-UP

"Getting my first cap was a really proud moment. Playing against Canada, a tough side, and in a full-strength England team was a cool moment for me and a great introduction to international rugby. That was really when the switch flipped. Before, I'd been very relaxed about it, but I knew at that point that I wanted to fight for my shirt every week."

It's been a whirlwind two years for Sadia, who has already cemented her place in the Red Roses squad since making her England debut in 2021. Last season, she also picked up the Rugby Players' Association 'Allianz Premier 15s Player of the Year Award'. One thing's for sure: there's plenty more to come from Sadia, and we can't wait to see what the future holds for this talented young England flanker.

ENGLAND'S

To win one cap for your country is an extraordinary achievement. To win 100 is the stuff of dreams… and reaching that milestone puts you in a very special club.

Only two players had ever reached the 100-cap mark in the entire history of the England Men's team: Jason Leonard and Ben Youngs. But during the 2022/23 season, two more players became England centurions: Owen Farrell and Dan Cole.

ENGLAND DEBUT
vs Scotland
at Murrayfield,
4 February 2012

ENGLAND CENTURION
vs New Zealand
at Twickenham,
19 November 2022

FARRELL

NEW CENTURIONS

ENGLAND DEBUT
vs Wales
at Twickenham,
6 February 2010

ENGLAND CENTURION
vs Ireland
at The Aviva Stadium,
18 March 2023

MEN'S 2022 AUTUMN

The Autumn Series is always one of the highlights of the rugby calendar and a chance for England to test themselves against some of the best teams on the planet.

Over four weeks in November, Argentina, Japan, New Zealand and South Africa all came to Twickenham to face England... and while one win, one draw and two defeats fell short of what we know the boys are capable of, there were still positives to take from this series.

England's opening fixtures were against two sides they will face again in Pool D at the Rugby World Cup: Argentina and Japan.

ENGLAND 29-30 ARGENTINA

Sunday 6 November

The Pumas picked up their first victory at Twickenham since 2006 with a one-point win in torrential rain. Joe Cokanasiga and Jack van Poortvliet scored for England, and Owen Farrell registered 100% from the kicking tee, but Emiliano Boffelli racked up 25 points to help see the visitors through by the narrowest of margins.

ENGLAND 52-13 JAPAN

Saturday 12 November

England bounced back in style a week later with a clinical performance against the Brave Blossoms of Japan. Marcus Smith and Guy Porter both crossed twice for England, with Freddie Steward and Ellis Genge also getting on the scoresheet. Just what the doctor ordered after a disappointing defeat. Next assignment: the All Blacks.

SERIES

ENGLAND 25-25 NEW ZEALAND

Saturday 19 November

There aren't many teams that could recover from 25-6 down against New Zealand with 10 minutes to go, but that's exactly what England did at Twickenham on 19 November, scoring three late tries to rescue an incredible draw. Check out the column on the right to relive England's dramatic fightback against the All Blacks.

ENGLAND 13-27 SOUTH AFRICA

Saturday 26 November

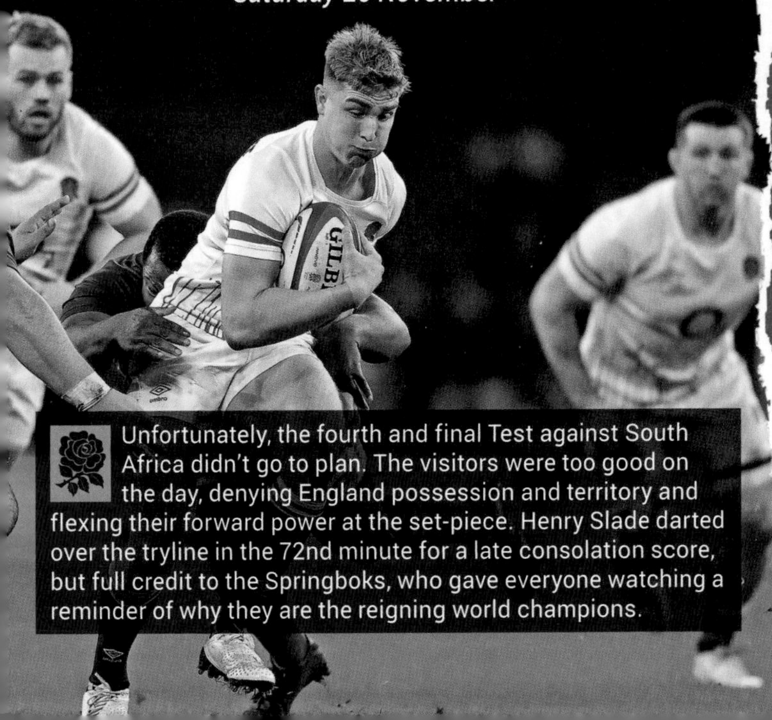

Unfortunately, the fourth and final Test against South Africa didn't go to plan. The visitors were too good on the day, denying England possession and territory and flexing their forward power at the set-piece. Henry Slade darted over the tryline in the 72nd minute for a late consolation score, but full credit to the Springboks, who gave everyone watching a reminder of why they are the reigning world champions.

10 CRAZY MINUTES AT TWICKENHAM

Here's how England produced a sensational late fightback to snatch a draw with the All Blacks

70' *England restart after a New Zealand drop goal, chasing a 19-point deficit with 10 minutes to play.*

71' ***Mako Vunipola*** *trucks the ball upfield before* ***Marcus Smith*** *prances through a gap and is dragged down just short of the line.*

72' ***Will Stuart*** *crashes over, but* ***Beauden Barrett*** *infringes and receives a yellow card, as England are awarded a penalty try.*

73' ***David Ribbans*** *breaks through the New Zealand midfield and offloads to* ***Owen Farrell****, who unleashes* ***Freddie Steward*** *down the wing, and the Leicester Tigers flyer scores in the corner one phase later.*

75' ***Smith*** *slots a tricky conversion to bring England within seven points.*

78' ***Jonny May*** *collects a clearance kick and sets off into the New Zealand half. England work the ball wide, break down the right wing, and* ***Guy Porter*** *is brought down five metres short. Three phases later,* ***Stuart*** *hits the ball at pace and powers over, but referee Mathieu Raynal wants to check the grounding.*

79' *The TMO [Television Match Official] awards the try and Twickenham erupts.*

80' ***Smith*** *slots the conversion and England are level.*

81' *Richie Mo'unga restarts, England snatch the ball at the breakdown and Smith boots it out from inside the 22 to end an incredible game of rugby.*

Unbelievable spirit from the boys. If there's one lesson to be learnt here, it's this: no matter what the score is, never give up!

WHAT A DAY AT

Yep, you read that right: "Queensholm", not "Kingsholm", after Gloucester Rugby renamed their stadium for the Allianz Premier 15s Final. Nice touch!

After one of the most exciting seasons in recent memory, Gloucester-Hartpury were crowned champions of England, becoming the first club outside of London to win the Premier 15s. The Cherry and Whites beat the Exeter Chiefs 34-19 in front of nearly 10,000 fans to end Harlequins and Saracens' recent dominance of the league, and the atmosphere at Queensholm that day was electric.

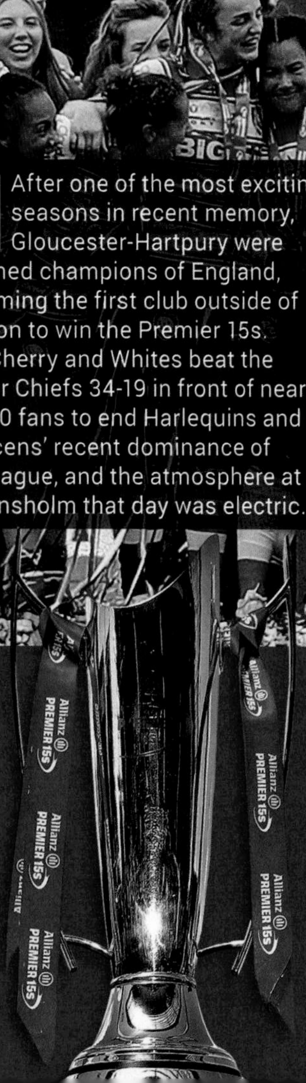

A NEW HORIZON

It's fair to say the Allianz Premier 15s has captured the imagination of rugby fans everywhere over the last six years, but it's time for a change. The women's top league now has a new name: Premiership Women's Rugby.

PWR
PREMIERSHIP WOMEN'S RUGBY

QUEENSHOLM!

England's Red Roses all play in this competition, but the league is also a home-from-home for some of the best players from around the world, with stars like the USA's Kate Zackary (Ealing Trailfinders), Spain's Laura Delgado (Gloucester-Hartpury) and Australia's Bella McKenzie (Harlequins) bringing plenty of international skill.

Eight of the ten teams will remain the same, with Wasps and DMP Sharks making way for Ealing Trailfinders and Leicester Tigers, and when you look at some of the stellar signings the newbies have already made (such as Abby Dow to Trailfinders and Amy Cokayne to Tigers) this incredible league is set to become more competitive than ever before!

PUZZLES

RUGBY WORLD CUP: LAST TIME OUT

Excitement levels are at an all-time high ahead of Rugby World Cup 2023 in France, but how much do you remember about England's last appearance on the game's biggest stage, back in 2019? Let's find out!

1 Where was Rugby World Cup 2019 held?

A. Australia B. Japan C. USA

2 Who captained England at the tournament?

A. Dan Cole B. Ben Youngs C. Owen Farrell

3 Why was England's pool game against France cancelled?

A. Because of a typhoon

B. Because several England players had colds

C. Because France's kitman brought the wrong shirts

4 As well as France, England were in Pool C with Tonga, the USA and...

A. Argentina B. Romania C. Fiji

5 England beat Australia in the quarter-finals, but what was the score?

A. 19-17 B. 34-20 C. 40-16

6 England responded to New Zealand's Haka in the semi-finals by lining up in which shape?

A. E B. W C. V

7 Who scored England's only try in the stunning 19-7 win against New Zealand?

A. Manu Tuilagi

B. Jonny May C. George Ford

8 In total, how many times have England and South Africa met in a Rugby World Cup Final?

A. Once B. Twice C. Three Times

9 Which England player won more turnovers than anyone else at the tournament?

A. Maro Itoje B. George Kruis

C. Sam Underhill

10 What was the name of the stadium that hosted the Rugby World Cup 2019 Final?

A. International Stadium Yokohama

B. Sapporo Dome C. Tokyo Stadium

SPOT THE BALL

It's one of the most unforgettable matches from the last Rugby World Cup, but can you spot the ball?

SPOTLIGHT ON:

RUGBY WORLD CUP 2023

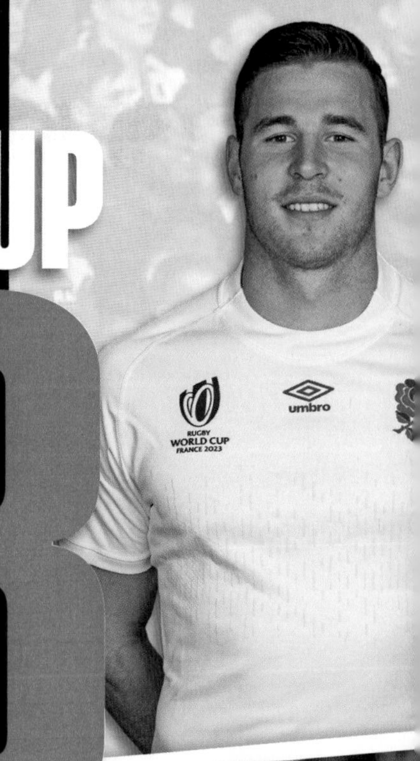

The 10th edition of the Rugby World Cup kicks off on 8 September in France, and we cannot wait!

Whether you're there in person or watching from home, we'll all be cheering England on in France and hoping they can go one step further this time and bring the Webb Ellis Cup back home. Come on boys!

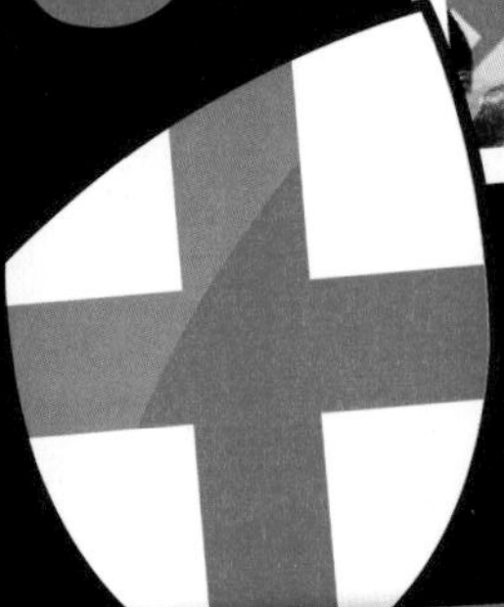

England are in Pool D alongside Japan, Argentina, Samoa and Chile, who are making their first-ever appearance at a Rugby World Cup. (Check out our complete list of Rugby World Cup fixtures on page 6.)

Here in England, we're lucky not just to have some of the best players in the world but some of the best fans too! Whether it's Murrayfield or Marseille, Sydney or Saint-Denis, England fans follow their team on the road, no matter where they play. Talk about passion!

ENGLAND'S RECORD

AT THE RUGBY WORLD CUP

England have played at every Rugby World Cup since the first tournament back in 1987. But do you know how they got on? Here's the lowdown.

1987

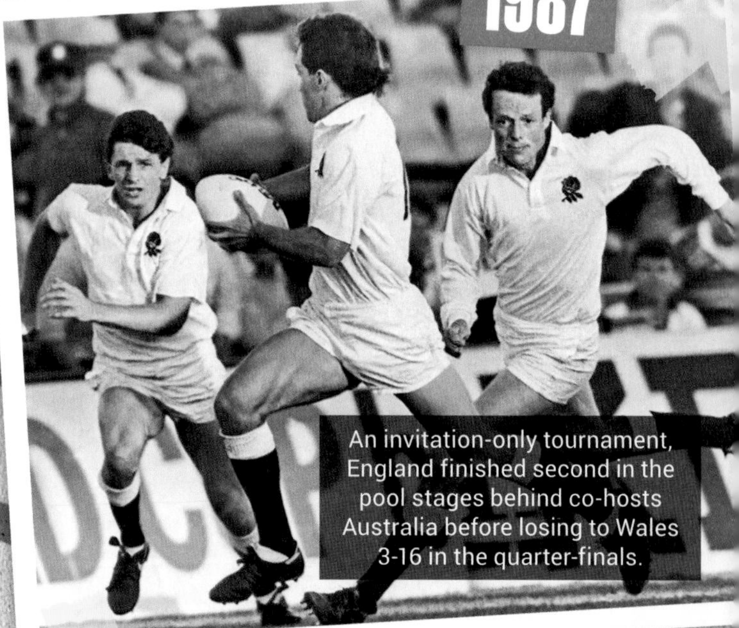

An invitation-only tournament, England finished second in the pool stages behind co-hosts Australia before losing to Wales 3-16 in the quarter-finals.

1991

Another second-place finish in the pool stages, this time behind New Zealand, but England reached the final with wins over France and Scotland in the knock-out stages before losing 6-12 to Australia in the final at Twickenham.

1995

Three wins from three in the group stages, followed by a dramatic late victory against Australia in the quarter-finals, but a New Zealand team, inspired by their winger Jonah Lomu, brought England's tournament to an end in the semi-finals.

1999

England posted thumping wins over Italy and Tonga, either side of a 16-30 loss to the All Blacks. After a tricky play-off against Fiji, England met South Africa at Twickenham for the quarter-finals, but were undone by fly-half Jannie De Beer, who kicked an astonishing five drop goals to knock England out.

2003

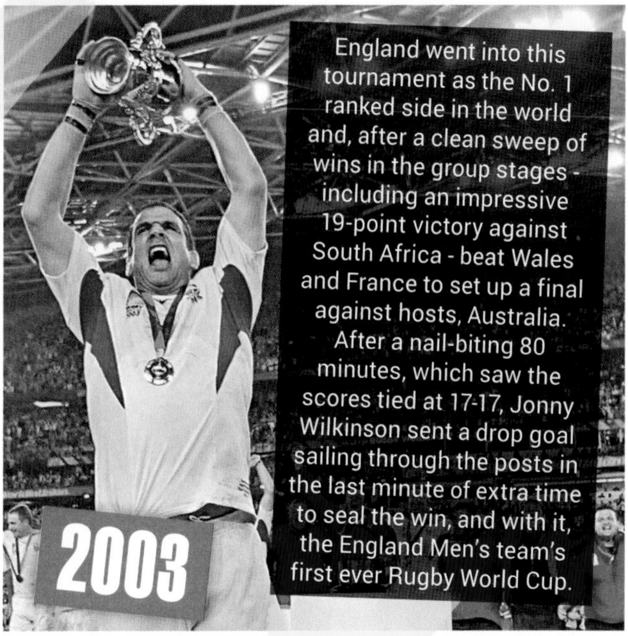

England went into this tournament as the No. 1 ranked side in the world and, after a clean sweep of wins in the group stages - including an impressive 19-point victory against South Africa - beat Wales and France to set up a final against hosts, Australia. After a nail-biting 80 minutes, which saw the scores tied at 17-17, Jonny Wilkinson sent a drop goal sailing through the posts in the last minute of extra time to seal the win, and with it, the England Men's team's first ever Rugby World Cup.

2007

After a slow start in the group stages, England's tournament kicked into life with a 10-12 quarter-final win against Australia. England went on to upset the hosts, France, in the semi-finals but narrowly lost a tense final 6-15 to South Africa.

2011

England topped their group with narrow wins over Argentina and Scotland, but a quarter-final showdown with France saw Les Bleus get revenge for their semi-final defeat four years earlier, knocking Martin Johnson's side out with a 12-19 win in Auckland.

2015

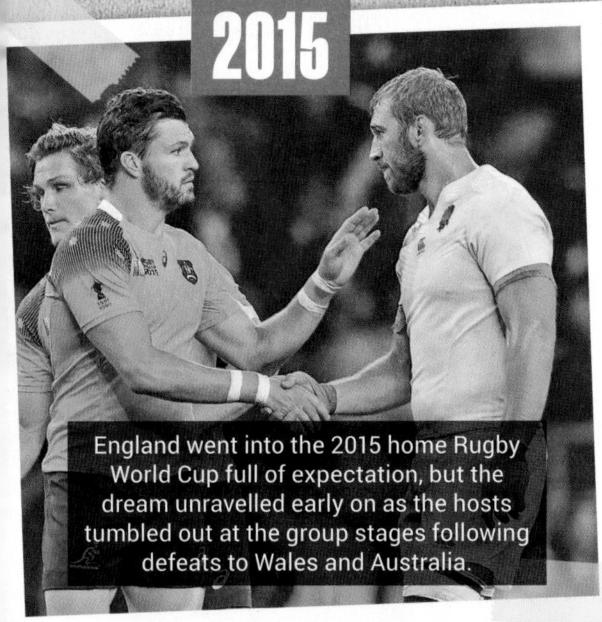

England went into the 2015 home Rugby World Cup full of expectation, but the dream unravelled early on as the hosts tumbled out at the group stages following defeats to Wales and Australia.

2019

After sailing through the group stages, England beat Australia in the quarter-finals to set up a semi-final against the in-form New Zealand, and produced a stunning performance to defeat the mighty All Blacks 19-7. The final would prove to be a different story, though, with South Africa running out 32-12 winners, including 22-points from Handré Pollard.

THE BIGGEST RUGBY PARTY IN ENGLAND

Twickenham hosted the finale of the HSBC World Rugby Sevens series over the weekend of 20 and 21 May, as over 75,000 fans came to The Home of England Rugby for a weekend of fun, fancy dress, live music and exhilarating Rugby Sevens.

ANOTHER YEAR. ANOTHER UNFORGETTABLE WEEKEND OF SEVENS.

England had plenty of stars representing the Great Britain side that weekend but finished in eighth place, while Argentina secured the 2023 HSBC London Sevens title with a thrilling win against Fiji in the final and New Zealand celebrated becoming overall Series Champions.

2022/23 MATCH RESULTS

2022 MEN'S AUTUMN NATIONS SERIES

ENGLAND 29 - 30 ARGENTINA
Sunday 6 November, *Twickenham Stadium*

ENGLAND 52 - 13 JAPAN
Saturday 12 November, *Twickenham Stadium*

ENGLAND 25 - 25 NEW ZEALAND
Saturday 19 November, *Twickenham Stadium*

ENGLAND 13 - 27 SOUTH AFRICA
Saturday 26 November, *Twickenham Stadium*

2023 MEN'S SIX NATIONS

ENGLAND 23 - 29 SCOTLAND
Saturday 4 February, *Twickenham Stadium*

ENGLAND 31 - 14 ITALY
Sunday 12 February, *Twickenham Stadium*

WALES 10 - 20 ENGLAND
Saturday 25 February, *Principality Stadium*

ENGLAND 10 - 53 FRANCE
Saturday 11 March, *Twickenham Stadium*

IRELAND 29 - 16 ENGLAND
Saturday 18 March, *Aviva Stadium*

2022 WOMEN'S RUGBY WORLD CUP

FIJI 19 - 84 ENGLAND
Saturday 8 October, *Eden Park*

FRANCE 7 - 13 ENGLAND
Saturday 15 October, *Northland Events Centre*

ENGLAND 75 - 0 SOUTH AFRICA
Sunday 23 October, *Waitakere Stadium*

ENGLAND 41 - 5 AUSTRALIA
Sunday 30 October, *Waitakere Stadium*

CANADA 19 - 26 ENGLAND
Saturday 5 November, *Eden Park*

NEW ZEALAND 34 - 31 ENGLAND
Saturday 12 November, *Eden Park*

2023 WOMEN'S SIX NATIONS

ENGLAND 58 - 7 SCOTLAND
Saturday 25 March, *Kingston Park*

ENGLAND 68 - 5 ITALY
Sunday 2 April, *Franklin's Gardens*

WALES 3 - 59 ENGLAND
Saturday 15 April, *Cardiff Arms Park*

IRELAND 0 - 48 ENGLAND
Saturday 22 April, *Musgrave Park*

ENGLAND 38 - 33 FRANCE
Saturday 29 April, *Twickenham Stadium*

ENGLAND MEN'S SQUAD

FORWARDS » PROP › HOOKER › FLANKER › LOCK › NO.8

JAMIE BLAMIRE

Position: Hooker
Date of Birth: 22 Dec 1997
Height: 1.85m
Weight: 113kg
Caps: 6
Club: Newcastle Falcons

OLLIE CHESSUM

Position: Lock
Date of Birth: 6 Sep 2000
Height: 2.00m
Weight: 118kg
Caps: 9
Club: Leicester Tigers

DAN COLE

Position: Prop
Date of Birth: 9 May 1987
Height: 1.91m
Weight: 118kg
Caps: 100
Club: Leicester Tigers

TOM CURRY

Position: Flanker
Date of Birth: 15 Jun 1998
Height: 1.85m
Weight: 110kg
Caps: 45
Club: Sale Sharks

THEO DAN

Position: Hooker
Date of Birth: 26 Dec 2000
Height: 1.79m
Weight: 102kg
Caps: 0
Club: Saracens

ALEX DOMBRANDT

Position: No. 8
Date of Birth: 29 Apr 1997
Height: 1.91m
Weight: 118kg
Caps: 14
Club: Harlequins

*Stats correct to August 2023

BEN EARL

Position: Flanker
Date of Birth: 7 Jan 1998
Height: 1.86m
Weight: 102kg
Caps: 6
Club: Saracens

ELLIS GENGE

Position: Prop
Date of Birth: 16 Feb 1995
Height: 1.86m
Weight: 117kg
Caps: 48
Club: Bristol Bears

JAMIE GEORGE

Position: Hooker
Date of Birth: 20 Oct 1990
Height: 1.83m
Weight: 114kg
Caps: 77
Club: Saracens

JONNY HILL

Position: Lock
Date of Birth: 8 Jun 1994
Height: 2.01m
Weight: 112kg
Caps: 19
Club: Sale Sharks

MARO ITOJE

Position: Lock
Date of Birth: 28 Oct 1994
Height: 1.95m
Weight: 115kg
Caps: 67
Club: Saracens

COURTNEY LAWES

Position: Lock
Date of Birth: 23 Feb 1989
Height: 2.01m
Weight: 115kg
Caps: 97
Club: Northampton Saints

LEWIS LUDLAM

Position: Flanker
Date of Birth: 8 Dec 1995
Height: 1.92m
Weight: 104kg
Caps: 19
Club: Northampton Saints

JOE MARLER

Position: Prop
Date of Birth: 7 Jul 1990
Height: 1.83m
Weight: 114kg
Caps: 79
Club: Harlequins

GEORGE MARTIN

Position: Lock
Date of Birth: 18 Jun 2001
Height: 1.98m
Weight: 118kg
Caps: 1
Club: Leicester Tigers

*Stats correct to August 2023

TOM PEARSON

Position: Flanker
Date of Birth: 26 Oct 1999
Height: 1.91m
Weight: 114kg
Caps: 0
Club: Northampton Saints

VAL RAPAVA-RUSKIN

Position: Prop
Date of Birth: 12 Oct 1992
Height: 1.91m
Weight: 124kg
Caps: 0
Club: Gloucester

DAVID RIBBANS

Position: Lock
Date of Birth: 29 Aug 1995
Height: 2.02m
Weight: 116kg
Caps: 4
Club: Toulon

BEVAN RODD

Position: Prop
Date of Birth: 26 Aug 2000
Height: 1.83m
Weight: 118kg
Caps: 2
Club: Sale Sharks

KYLE SINCKLER

Position: Prop
Date of Birth: 30 Mar 1993
Height: 1.83m
Weight: 120kg
Caps: 61
Club: Bristol Bears

WILL STUART

Position: Prop
Date of Birth: 12 Jul 1996
Height: 1.88m
Weight: 132kg
Caps: 25
Club: Bath

SAM UNDERHILL

Position: Flanker
Date of Birth: 22 Jul 1996
Height: 1.86m
Weight: 103kg
Caps: 29
Club: Bath

BILLY VUNIPOLA

Position: No. 8
Date of Birth: 3 Nov 1992
Height: 1.88m
Weight: 130kg
Caps: 68
Club: Saracens

MAKO VUNIPOLA

Position: Prop
Date of Birth: 14 Jan 1991
Height: 1.80m
Weight: 126kg
Caps: 79
Club: Saracens

*Stats correct to August 2023

ENGLAND MEN'S SQUAD

BACKS » SCRUM HALF › FLY HALF › CENTRE › WING › FULL BACK

JACK WALKER

Position: Hooker
Date of Birth: 6 May 1996
Height: 1.86m
Weight: 101kg
Caps: 3
Club: Harlequins

HENRY ARUNDELL

Position: Full back
Date of Birth: 8 Nov 2002
Height: 1.83m
Weight: 98kg
Caps: 7
Club: Racing 92

JACK WILLIS

Position: Flanker
Date of Birth: 24 Dec 1996
Height: 1.90m
Weight: 110kg
Caps: 10
Club: Toulouse

DANNY CARE

Position: Scrum half
Date of Birth: 2 Jan 1987
Height: 1.77m
Weight: 87kg
Caps: 87
Club: Harlequins

TOM WILLIS

Position: No. 8
Date of Birth: 18 Jan 1999
Height: 1.92m
Weight: 120kg
Caps: 0
Club: Saracens

JOE COKANASIGA

Position: Wing
Date of Birth: 15 Nov 1997
Height: 1.92m
Weight: 112kg
Caps: 14
Club: Bath

*Stats correct to August 2023

ELLIOT DALY

Position: Full back
Date of Birth: 8 Oct 1992
Height: 1.85m
Weight: 98kg
Caps: 57
Club: Saracens

OWEN FARRELL

Position: Fly half
Date of Birth: 24 Sep 1991
Height: 1.88m
Weight: 94kg
Caps: 106
Club: Saracens

GEORGE FORD

Position: Fly half
Date of Birth: 16 Mar 1993
Height: 1.78m
Weight: 86kg
Caps: 81
Club: Sale Sharks

OLLIE LAWRENCE

Position: Centre
Date of Birth: 18 Sep 1999
Height: 1.80m
Weight: 100kg
Caps: 11
Club: Bath

MAX MALINS

Position: Full back
Date of Birth: 7 Jan 1997
Height: 1.82m
Weight: 88kg
Caps: 18
Club: Bristol Bears

JOE MARCHANT

Position: Centre
Date of Birth: 16 Jul 1996
Height: 1.83m
Weight: 89kg
Caps: 15
Club: Stade Français

JONNY MAY

Position: Wing
Date of Birth: 1 Apr 1990
Height: 1.88m
Weight: 90kg
Caps: 72
Club: Gloucester

CADAN MURLEY

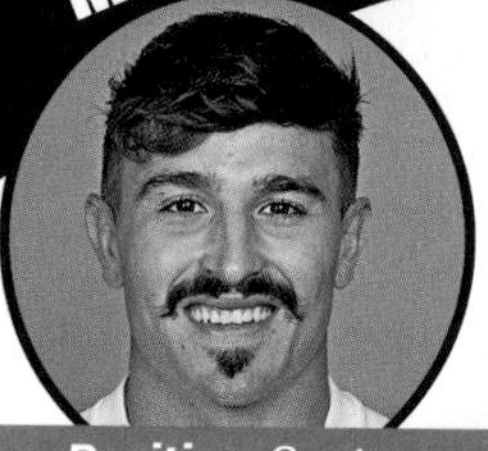

Position: Centre
Date of Birth: 31 Jul 1999
Height: 1.77m
Weight: 92kg
Caps: 0
Club: Harlequins

*Stats correct to August 2023

GUY PORTER

Position: Centre
Date of Birth: 23 Jan 1997
Height: 1.86m
Weight: 96kg
Caps: 4
Club: Leicester Tigers

HENRY SLADE

Position: Centre
Date of Birth: 19 Mar 1993
Height: 1.91m
Weight: 96kg
Caps: 56
Club: Exeter Chiefs

MARCUS SMITH

Position: Fly half
Date of Birth: 14 Feb 1999
Height: 1.75m
Weight: 82kg
Caps: 21
Club: Harlequins

FREDDIE STEWARD

Position: Full back
Date of Birth: 5 Dec 2000
Height: 1.96m
Weight: 107kg
Caps: 8
Club: Leicester Tigers

MANU TUILAGI

Position: Centre
Date of Birth: 18 May 1991
Height: 1.85m
Weight: 111kg
Caps: 51
Club: Sale Sharks

JACK VAN POORTVLIET

Position: Scrum half
Date of Birth: 15 May 2001
Height: 1.83m
Weight: 84kg
Caps: 12
Club: Leicester Tigers

ANTHONY WATSON

Position: Full back
Date of Birth: 26 Feb 1994
Height: 1.85m
Weight: 93kg
Caps: 55
Club: Unattached

BEN YOUNGS

Position: Scrum half
Date of Birth: 5 Sep 1989
Height: 1.78m
Weight: 88kg
Caps: 122
Club: Leicester Tigers

*Stats correct to August 2023

ENGLAND WOMEN'S SQUAD

FORWARDS » PROP › HOOKER › FLANKER › LOCK › NO.8

ZOE ALDCROFT

Position: Lock
Date of Birth: 19 Nov 1996
Height: 1.81m
Weight: 85kg
Caps: 43
Club: Gloucester-Hartpury

SARAH BECKETT

Position: No. 8
Date of Birth: 14 Feb 1999
Height: 1.78m
Weight: 96kg
Caps: 30
Club: Gloucester-Hartpury

SARAH BERN

Position: Prop
Date of Birth: 10 Jul 1997
Height: 1.70m
Weight: 91kg
Caps: 57
Club: Bristol Bears

HANNAH BOTTERMAN

Position: Prop
Date of Birth: 8 Jun 1999
Height: 1.58m
Weight: 103kg
Caps: 37
Club: Bristol Bears

MACKENZIE CARSON

Position: Prop
Date of Birth: 9 Mar 2002
Height: 1.70m
Weight: 90kg
Caps: 5
Club: Gloucester-Hartpury

POPPY CLEALL

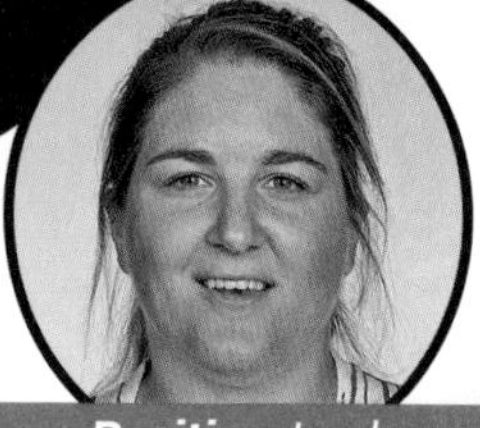

Position: Lock
Date of Birth: 12 Jun 1992
Height: 1.81m
Weight: 96kg
Caps: 65
Club: Saracens

*Stats correct to August 2023

KELSEY CLIFFORD

Position: Prop

Date of Birth: 11 Dec 2001

Height: 1.68m

Weight: 105kg

Caps: 2

Club: Saracens

AMY COKAYNE

Position: Hooker

Date of Birth: 11 Jul 1996

Height: 1.67m

Weight: 86kg

Caps: 72

Club: Leicester Tigers

VICKII CORNBOROUGH

Position: Prop

Date of Birth: 3 Mar 1990

Height: 1.68m

Weight: 87kg

Caps: 75

Club: Harlequins

*Stats correct to August 2023

LARK DAVIES

Position: Hooker
Date of Birth: 3 Mar 1995
Height: 1.62m
Weight: 85kg
Caps: 49
Club: Bristol Bears

ROSIE GALLIGAN

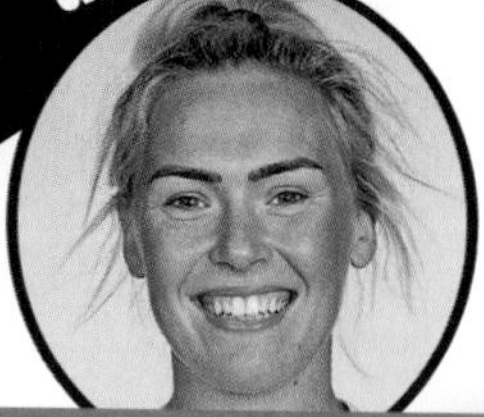

Position: Lock
Date of Birth: 30 Apr 1998
Height: 1.75m
Weight: 85kg
Caps: 10
Club: Saracens

SADIA KABEYA

Position: Flanker
Date of Birth: 22 Feb 2002
Height: 1.70m
Weight: 84kg
Caps: 13
Club: Loughborough Lightning

ALEX MATTHEWS

Position: Flanker
Date of Birth: 3 Aug 1993
Height: 1.73m
Weight: 81kg
Caps: 59
Club: Gloucester-Hartpury

MAUD MUIR

Position: Prop
Date of Birth: 12 Jul 2001
Height: 1.67m
Weight: 82kg
Caps: 20
Club: Gloucester-Hartpury

CATHERINE O'DONNELL

Position: Lock
Date of Birth: 13 Jun 1996
Height: 1.81m
Weight: 93kg
Caps: 27
Club: Loughborough Lightning

MARLIE PACKER

Position: Flanker
Date of Birth: 2 Oct 1989
Height: 1.65m
Weight: 78kg
Caps: 94
Club: Saracens

*Stats correct to August 2023

ENGLAND WOMEN'S SQUAD

BACKS » SCRUM HALF › FLY HALF › CENTRE › WING › FULL BACK

CONNIE POWELL

Position: Hooker
Date of Birth: 13 Jul 2000
Height: 1.65m
Weight: 88kg
Caps: 9
Club: Harlequins

HOLLY AITCHISON

Position: Centre
Date of Birth: 13 Sep 1997
Height: 1.75m
Weight: 69kg
Caps: 20
Club: Bristol Bears

MORWENNA TALLING

Position: Flanker
Date of Birth: 5 Aug 2002
Height: 1.85m
Weight: 84kg
Caps: 7
Club: Sale Sharks

JESSICA BREACH

Position: Wing
Date of Birth: 4 Nov 1997
Height: 1.68m
Weight: 73kg
Caps: 28
Club: Saracens

ABBIE WARD

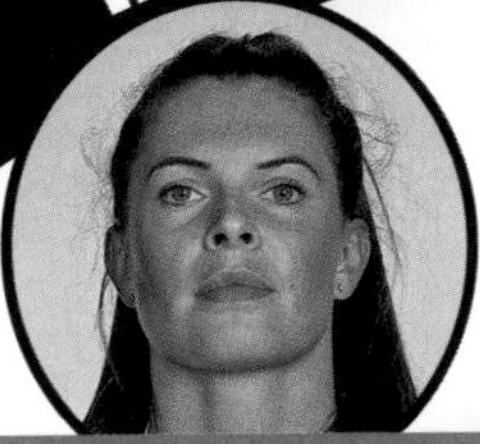

Position: Lock
Date of Birth: 27 Mar 1993
Height: 1.81m
Weight: 86kg
Caps: 61
Club: Bristol Bears

ABIGAIL DOW

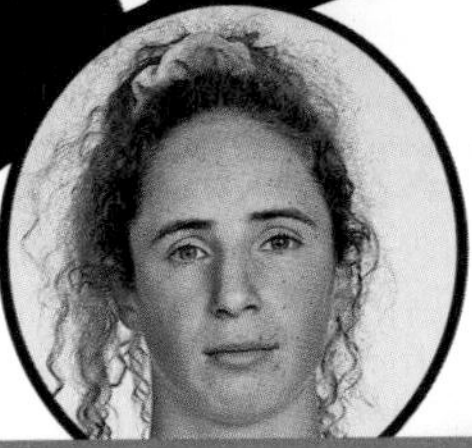

Position: Wing
Date of Birth: 29 Sep 1997
Height: 1.68m
Weight: 72kg
Caps: 35
Club: Ealing Trailfinders

*Stats correct to August 2023

ZOE HARRISON

Position: Fly half
Date of Birth: 14 Apr 1998
Height: 1.73m
Weight: 73kg
Caps: 46
Club: Saracens

TATYANA HEARD

Position: Centre
Date of Birth: 14 Jan 1995
Height: 1.64m
Weight: 75kg
Caps: 14
Club: Gloucester-Hartpury

ELLIE KILDUNNE

Position: Wing
Date of Birth: 8 Sep 1999
Height: 1.76m
Weight: 68kg
Caps: 34
Club: Harlequins

CLAUDIA MACDONALD

Position: Scrum half
Date of Birth: 4 Jan 1996
Height: 1.67m
Weight: 65kg
Caps: 28
Club: Exeter Chiefs

LUCY PACKER

Position: Scrum half
Date of Birth: 2 Feb 2000
Height: 1.61m
Weight: 55kg
Caps: 14
Club: Harlequins

AMBER REED

Position: Centre
Date of Birth: 3 Apr 1991
Height: 1.78m
Weight: 85kg
Caps: 65
Club: Bristol Bears

*Stats correct to August 2023

HELENA ROWLAND

Position: *Fly half*
Date of Birth: 19 Sep 1999
Height: 1.68m
Weight: 66kg
Caps: 24
Club: Loughborough Lightning

EMILY SCARRATT

Position: *Centre*
Date of Birth: 8 Feb 1990
Height: 1.81m
Weight: 81kg
Caps: 108
Club: Loughborough Lightning

EMMA SING

Position: *Full back*
Date of Birth: 11 Mar 2001
Height: 1.78m
Weight: 73kg
Caps: 5
Club: Gloucester -Hartpury

*Stats correct to August 2023

QUIZ ANSWERS

And finally – the answers! How good was your rugby knowledge? Find out now!

THE AMAZING RUGBY WORDSEARCH

» PAGE 18

Z	G	E	G	Z	S	R	A	X	K	V	L	E	L	L	I	S	G	E	N	G	E	T	F	L	M	M	O	K
M	V	Y	K	R	K	P	T	N	W	I	D	P	T	K	F	K	Y	Z	J	C	W	V	Z	T	X	Q	R	G
S	T	I	E	Q	Q	R	W	T	R	I	M	O	U	V	D	A	Q	T	N	C	X	C	R	C	K	S	J	A
O	F	E	G	Z	N	W	W	M	Q	U	M	J	R	F	D	D	Y	E	I	K	S	U	F	J	E	L	D	W
Z	B	G	J	O	R	T	Q	C	W	Z	B	N	N	U	H	C	T	Q	N	R	Z	A	Z	C	P	R	G	S
Q	Z	H	O	F	B	I	O	Q	S	M	A	W	O	U	W	I	R	L	C	N	V	A	R	H	A	F	S	I
Y	E	N	H	W	A	A	U	L	A	M	A	M	V	M	C	S	I	I	S	I	L	Z	J	W	M	L	M	B
Z	X	X	N	K	T	Z	P	G	S	S	F	U	E	I	B	R	D	P	E	V	D	C	E	I	J	I	O	X
Z	Z	X	M	E	I	U	Z	E	C	L	B	W	R	P	P	D	U	M	C	V	K	T	S	P	W	U	H	I
O	V	M	I	D	J	F	N	L	F	L	I	T	L	Z	F	X	I	H	T	T	S	B	Z	Z	V	D	U	Q
E	L	A	T	K	H	I	R	W	T	K	Z	S	A	C	L	T	H	A	I	E	D	H	V	N	W	V	N	W
A	H	F	C	S	L	A	H	X	M	Z	V	A	U	R	L	R	H	B	I	V	M	W	U	O	B	L	T	B
L	Q	Y	H	J	K	D	S	N	V	S	O	I	U	L	O	R	G	D	F	Q	S	M	Q	X	L	Z	H	W
D	J	L	E	A	R	I	C	J	N	V	U	P	U	N	D	Z	D	O	W	E	N	F	A	R	R	E	L	L
C	Q	T	L	L	Q	A	W	A	X	Y	V	F	E	U	V	E	S	C	H	A	M	P	I	O	N	S	Z	Z
R	Z	T	L	T	D	E	R	S	V	G	P	O	K	H	R	Z	W	O	R	L	D	R	E	C	O	R	D	E
O	J	B	Q	W	I	V	B	P	P	C	K	F	L	F	E	T	F	D	T	P	E	U	E	Z	W	H	E	E
F	J	M	S	A	D	I	A	K	A	B	E	Y	A	U	U	Q	E	Q	T	J	I	F	H	R	J	K	T	B
T	L	Q	W	J	Y	H	L	S	R	R	L	B	H	B	F	W	F	I	O	J	K	C	J	O	Q	P	B	V
S	E	H	F	M	V	V	D	Z	B	R	Z	Y	E	E	D	I	E	J	E	C	G	A	X	L	I	Y	D	I
J	S	Q	B	U	I	B	F	N	Q	V	P	D	P	E	N	A	L	T	Y	P	B	V	B	O	T	C	S	S
Q	K	I	C	K	O	F	F	G	D	C	W	V	F	W	J	O	J	P	D	O	Y	J	P	L	S	X	W	B
R	R	B	Y	J	I	W	G	R	A	N	D	S	L	A	M	U	K	M	M	D	F	D	G	G	Q	D	T	G
S	Z	J	B	P	N	H	A	S	T	E	V	E	B	O	R	T	H	W	I	C	K	F	L	P	F	B	I	G
C	A	P	T	A	I	N	N	K	D	R	E	D	R	O	S	E	S	L	V	M	Y	C	J	Y	Q	L	H	V
J	D	X	C	X	V	Z	B	A	L	L	B	H	R	O	K	V	H	F	M	G	B	Q	U	G	M	T	L	O
W	H	T	M	M	G	D	U	E	Y	H	S	F	G	I	I	K	L	I	I	S	O	L	R	C	I	D	H	E

WHO AM I?

» PAGE 19

Freddie Steward

RUGBY WORLD CUP: LAST TIME OUT

» PAGE 38

1. B, 2. C, 3. A, 4. A, 5. C, 6. C, 7. A, 8. B, 9. A, 10. A

4

WHERE'S FAZ?

We've dropped England skipper Owen Farrell into the crowd. Can you find him?